Campfire Songs,
Ballads,
and Lullabies

Folk Music

North American Folklore for Youth

Campfire Songs, Ballads, and Lullabies

Folk Music

Gus Snedeker

Mason Crest

Mason Crest
370 Reed Road
Broomall, Pennsylvania 19008
www.masoncrest.com

Printed and bound in the United States of America.

First printing
9 8 7 6 5 4 3 2 1

Library of Congress Cataloging-in-Publication Data

Snedeker, Gus.
 Campfire songs, ballads, and lullabies : folk music / Gus Snedeker.
     p. cm. — (North American folklore for youth)
 Includes index.
 ISBN 978-1-4222-2492-2 (hardcover) — ISBN 978-1-4222-2486-1 (hardcover series) — ISBN 978-1-4222-9257-0 (ebook)
 1. Folk music—History and criticism—Juvenile literature. [1. Folk music.] I. Title.
 ML3545.S66 2012
 781.62'13—dc23

                         2012013557

Produced by Harding House Publishing Services, Inc.
www.hardinghousepages.com
Cover design by Torque Advertising + Design.

Contents

✳ Introduction

by Dr. Alan Jabbour

What do a story, a joke, a fiddle tune, a quilt, a dance, a game of jacks, a holiday celebration, and a Halloween costume have in common? Not much, at first glance. But they're all part of the stuff we call "folklore."

The word "folklore" means the ways of thinking and acting that are learned and passed along by ordinary people. Folklore goes from grandparents to parents to children—and on to *their* children. It may be passed along in words, like the urban legend we hear from friends who promise us that it *really* happened to someone they know. Or it may be tunes or dance steps we pick up on the block where we live. It could be the quilt our aunt made. Much of the time we learn folklore without even knowing where or how we learned it.

Folklore is not something that's far away or long ago. It's something we use and enjoy every day! It is often ordinary—

and yet at the same time, it makes life seem very special. Folklore is the culture we share with others in our homes, our neighborhoods, and our places of worship. It helps tell us who we are.

Our first sense of who we are comes from our families. Family folklore—like eating certain meals together or prayers or songs—gives us a sense of belonging. But as we grow older we learn to belong to other groups as well. Maybe your family is Irish. Or maybe you live in a Hispanic neighborhood in New York City. Or you might live in the country in the middle of Iowa. Maybe you're a Catholic—or a Muslim—or you're Jewish. Each one of these groups to which you belong will have it's own folklore. A certain dance step may be African American. A story may have come from Germany. A hymn may be Protestant. A recipe may have been handed down by your Italian grandmother. All this folklore helps the people who belong to a certain group feel connected to each other.

Folklore can make each group special, different from all the others. But at the same time folklore is one of the best ways we can get to know to each other. We can learn about Vietnamese immigrants by eating Vietnamese foods. We can understand newcomers from Somalia by enjoying their music and dance. Stories, songs, and artwork move from group to group. And everyone is the richer!

Folklore isn't something you usually learn in school. Somebody, somewhere, taught you that jump-rope rhyme you know—but you probably can't remember *who* taught you. You definitely didn't learn it in a schoolbook, though! You can study folklore and learn about it—that's what you are doing now in this book!—but folklore normally is something that just gets passed along from person to person.

This series of books explores the many kinds folklore you can find across the North American continent. As you read, you'll learn something about yourself—and you'll learn about your neighbors as well!

Songs that children sing while jumping rope are one kind of folk song.

✳ ONE
What Is Folk Music?

Words to Understand

Someone who is a *professional* gets paid for doing what she does.

A *generation* is all the people born at about the same time. Your grandparents are one generation, your parents and aunts and uncles are another generation, and you, your brothers and sisters, and your cousins are another.

ave you ever sung "Miss Mary Mack"?

> Miss Mary Mack, Mack, Mack
> All dressed in black, black, black
> With silver buttons, buttons, buttons
> All down her back, back, back.

She asked her mother, mother, mother
for fifty cents, cents, cents
To see the elephant, elephant, elephant
Jump over the fence, fence, fence.

He [or she or it] jumped so high, high, high
He reached the sky, sky, sky
He never came back, back, back
Till the 4th of July, ly, ly!

Could you say where you learned this song? Probably not. Or if you can, it was probably on the playground. Or maybe your older brother or sister taught it to you. It's a folk song.

We don't usually know who wrote folk songs. No one knows the composer's name. Whoever wrote the song or sang the song for the first time really doesn't matter. What matters is that it caught on. It spread from person to person. Then it was passed on from **generation** to generation. Each singer or musician hears a folk song from someone else.

Folk musicians don't usually learn songs that are written down. In fact, a lot of folk musicians can't even read music. Folk musicians are ordinary people. They aren't *professional* musicians. They didn't go to school for years to learn music. They just play folk music at home or for friends. And it's not just

Many songs that children are taught by their parents are folk songs.

musicians who pass along folk songs either. It's everybody—kids on the playground, families around the campfire, moms and dads singing lullabies to their children.

These days, though, folk music is actually written down sometimes. Otherwise, we might lose some of it if it doesn't get written down somewhere. With so many new songs being sung, some of the old ones might be forgotten. So if you go to your library, you'll find there are big books full of folk music.

But learning folk songs from other people still happens all the time. Folk music comes from lots of places.

Some old songs were sung while people worked. Some folk music is religious. It's a way to teach people about God. Or maybe it's a way to help people have faith when times are hard. Other folk songs tell stories. These kinds of songs are called ballads. A ballad might tell the story of a big disaster. Or maybe it tells about a war or a battle. Folk songs can be a way to hold on to memories—and then pass them along to others, including new generations.

Today, there are lots of kinds of music. We can listen to the latest hits on our mp3 player. Radios blast out music of all sorts. But folk music doesn't die. It's still there. If you listen closely, you might hear an old folk song in the middle of a modern hip-hop rap. And some of the modern songs being sung today may

ALAN LOMAX: A COLLECTOR OF FOLK SONGS

Alan Lomax and his father John Lomax collected American folk songs. They went on "collecting tours" all around the country. They recorded folk musicians playing their own songs. Those songs became a part of the American Folk-Song Archive. Later, Alan went to Great Britain, Italy, and Spain. He recorded the folk music in these countries too.

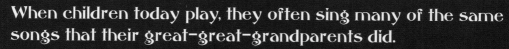

When children today play, they often sing many of the same songs that their great-great-grandparents did.

end up as folk music one day. People will forget who wrote them, but they'll still sing the songs. They'll still pass the songs along to their children and grandchildren.

Your great-grandchildren will be listening to very different music from what you enjoy today. But odds are good that they'll be still singing some of the very same songs your grandparents did!

Many folk songs were born in prisons.

✳ TWO
Folk Songs

There are all sorts of folk songs out there. Each sort has a different purpose. People of all ages and sorts sing folk songs. Folk music used to be the only music around.

Work Songs

Back in the old days, people worked a lot. Most people were farmers. They worked all day long. To make their days brighter, a lot of people sang. The songs they sang became folk music.

Other workers besides farmers made up songs too. There are songs about mining, cattle herding, and trucking. You probably know this one about working on the railroad:

> I've been working on the railroad
> All the livelong day.
> I've been working on the railroad
> Just to pass the time away.
>
> Don't you hear the whistle blowing,
> Rise up so early in the morn:
> Don't you hear the captain shouting,
> "Dinah, blow your horn!"

Music was a way to make hard work–like laying train rails–
seem easier.

Songs also helped African slaves get through their hard work in the fields. The music cheered them up. Their work kept time with the rhythm of the music. That made their work seem a little like dancing. It made it a little easier. Those songs became African American folk songs.

Here's one that talks about what the slaves faced:

Working all day,
And part of the night,
And up before the morning light.
When will Jehovah hear our cry,
And free the sons of Africa?

Women also sang songs about working at home. Now, many women work outside the home. In the past, though, most women worked at home, taking care of the family and the house. They made up their own songs to make their work go faster. This song teaches children about the cycle of a woman's week:

Here we go 'round the mulberry bush,
The mulberry bush, the mulberry bush,
Here we go 'round the mulberry bush,
So early in the morning.

This is the way we wash our clothes,
Wash our clothes, wash our clothes,
This is the way we wash our clothes,
So early Monday morning.

This is the way we iron our clothes,
Iron our clothes, iron our clothes,
This is the way we iron our clothes,
So early Tuesday morning.

This is the way we sweep the floor,
Sweep the floor, sweep the floor.
This is the way we sweep the floor,
So early Wednesday morning.

This is the way we mend our clothes,
Mend our clothes, mend our clothes.
This is the way we mend our clothes,
So early Thursday morning.

This is the way we clean the house,
Clean the house, clean the house,
This is the way we clean the house,
So early Friday morning.

This is the way we bake our bread,

Bake our bread, bake our bread,

This is the way we bake our bread,

So early Saturday morning.

This is the way we go to church,

Go to church, go to church,

This is the way we go to church,

So early Sunday morning.

Love Songs

Many folk songs talk about love, just like a lot of songs you hear on the radio today. Some folk songs talk about falling in love. Others tell about losing love. There are songs about not being able to find love.

Here's a love song about the awkwardness that comes with dating:

Johnson boys were raised in the ashes,

Didn't know how to court a maid,

Turn their backs and hide their faces,

Sight of a pretty girl makes 'em afraid.

Johnson boys they went a-courtin'.

Coon Creek girls so pretty and sweet,

They couldn't make no conversation,

They didn't know where to put their feet.

Religious Songs

Lots of folk songs have to do with religion. In the past, not many people could read or write. They couldn't read the Bible. So people sang songs to remind each other about God and to teach each other about religion. Religious folk songs are sometimes called hymns or spirituals.

In early America, religious meetings outside were common. Ministers preached to big crowds of people under tents. They were spreading the Christian message and inspiring people. These meetings always included music. Some of the meetings were mostly white people. Some were mostly black people. Some were both. Eventually, black and white spiritual music ended up getting mixed together.

Here's part of an African American spiritual song. There's a lot of repetition.

In that great getting up morning, fare thee well, fare thee well.

In that great getting up morning, fare thee well, fare thee well.

In that great getting up morning, fare thee well, fare thee well.

In that great getting up morning, fare thee well, fare thee well.

Oh preacher, fold your Bible, fare thee well, fare thee well.

Oh preacher, fold your Bible, fare thee well, fare thee well.

For the last souls converted, fare thee well, fare thee well.

Yes for the last souls converted, fare thee well, fare thee well.

Many folk songs started out being sung in churches. And many are still sung today in churches.

Protest Songs

Sometimes people sang when they needed courage. They wanted to protest something they thought was unfair. They used songs to help them.

During the Industrial Revolution, many people started working in factories instead of on farms. This meant that more people were working for bosses. The working conditions in the factories weren't very good. Workers had to work very long hours. Dangerous machines could hurt people. The pay wasn't very good.

During the Industrial Revolution, factory workers sang songs calling for change in their working conditions.

Some workers realized that if they joined together, things could be better. Together they could fight for better pay and hours. The groups workers formed were called unions. Folk songs were one way that unions protested. They sang about how horrible their jobs were. The songs spread the word to other workers. It was a way to pull workers together. Together they were stronger. They could fight to make changes.

In the twentieth century, folk singers used music to protest things the government was doing. They sang about war, especially the Vietnam War. Folk songs helped create a movement against the war. They helped change other people's minds. Songs inspired people to be brave and stand up for what they believed.

Prison Songs

People in prison sometimes ended up singing about it. Some prisoners had to work on chain gangs. Lots of prisoners worked together (chained together) to dig railroads or ditches. In the song below, the "huhs" were when prisoners swung their picks or hammers.

Look over yonder, huh!
Hot burning sun turning over
Look over yonder, huh!
Hot burning sun turning over

And it won't go down,

Oh my Lord, it won't go down.

Prisoners working with axes and singing.

Some folk song collectors think that prisons produced some of the best folk songs there are. Prisoners didn't have much else to do. Music helped them fight boredom. It helped make their work on chain gangs seem a little easier.

Children's Songs

Some folk songs helped kids learn. Kids still use songs to learn today. You probably learned your ABCs using the "Alphabet Song."

Songs for kids often include movements or clapping. Think of jump-rope rhymes or clapping games.

Lullabies soothe crying babies. Parents have been singing their babies to sleep for hundreds of years. One of the most famous lullabies is:

Hush little baby, don't say a word
Mama's gonna buy you a mockingbird.
And if that mockingbird don't sing,
Mama's gonna buy you a diamond ring.
And if that diamond ring is brass,
Mama's gonna buy you a looking glass.
And if that looking glass gets broke,
Mama's gonna buy you a billy goat.

Folk instruments help give folk music its special sound. A guitar with a metal resonator like that shown here is often used in bluegrass music.

✳ THREE
Folk Instruments

American folk music can be played on just about anything. But there are some instruments that folk musicians use more than others.

Folk musicians often made their own instruments. They couldn't go online or to the local music store. They had to create their own way of making music.

Today, you can buy folk instruments in lots of different places. Some are still handmade by American *craftspeople*.

Banjo

Banjo music is a type of American folk music. But the banjo didn't come from America at all. It started out in West Africa. The very first banjos were made from big gourds. They were covered with animal skin. Then four strings of silk or dried bird gut were added to the front.

The banjo is an American instrument that started out, long ago, in Africa.

A fiddle is the same thing as a violin. Folk musicians play violins a little differently, though.

The banjo made its way to the United States with slaves from West Africa. Early American banjos were made of gourds and wood. Eventually they became the banjos that we know today.

Fiddles

Fiddles are really just violins played by folk musicians. Violins are old instruments. You could find violins in the 1700s that were pretty much the same as violins today.

The fiddle is a very common instrument in all types of American folk music. Lots of *immigrants* brought them with them when they came to the New World.

APPALACHIA

The area around the Appalachian Mountains is called Appalachia. It stretches from Pennsylvania, to West Virginia, to Kentucky and Tennessee. It includes parts of other states too.

A certain kind of American folk music was born in Appalachia. The Europeans who settled there were Scottish families. The steep mountains kept the settlers separate from the rest of America for many years. They held on to old ways of doing things. They sang old songs from Scotland and Ireland. The echoes of those songs can still be heard in the folk music from Appalachia.

Fiddles are played differently in each region of the United States. Some fiddlers might tuck their fiddles into the crooks of their elbows. A fiddler from one area might saw on the instrument with a bow. Another would use long, smooth strokes with the bow.

Dulcimer

Dulcimers are also known as lap harps. They are mostly used for folk music from the Appalachian Mountains. They have

This is one kind of dulcimer.

three or four strings. They don't have a **standard** shape. They can be rectangular, oval, or teardrops.

Players lay the dulcimers on their laps. Then they play the strings with picks or with their fingers. The instrument sounds a little bit like bagpipes.

FOUR
Some History

All music has to come from somewhere. The folk music in North America has its roots in a lot of different places.

European folk music helped shaped American folk music. Music from Europe is all very similar. There are differences between different countries and areas, of course. But all European music shares some things in common.

Music from Eastern Asia or from Native Americans is very different. But these two types of music didn't influence American folk music very much.

Most of our folk music comes from Europe. Almost all of the immigrants who came to North America during the early years were from Europe. They came from different European countries. But they came from the same general area of the world.

A BLUES FOLK SONG

Men used to lay down rails and dig tunnels by hand to make railroads. Sometimes they told a story about a man named John Henry, who worked for the railroad. He was known for how strong he was. He bragged about how fast he could dig.

One day, the railroad company was working on a tunnel. At one end, the crew had a drill to make the tunnel. John Henry was on the other end. He bet that he could work faster than the drill. There was a contest. By the end of the day, John Henry won! But he died from working so hard.

The story inspired a ballad:

John Henry said to the captain,
I'm gonna take a little trip downtown,
Get me a 30-pound hammer with that nine-foot handle.
I'll beat your steam drill down,
I'll beat your steam drill down.

Now the man that invented the steam drill,
He thought he was mighty fine.
But John Henry drove 15 feet,

The steam drill made only 9,
The steam drill made only 9.

John hammered on the mountain,
Till his hammer was striking fire,
But he swung so hard he broke his heart,
And he laid down his hammer and he died,
He laid down his hammer and he died.

They took John Henry to the graveyard,
Laid him down in the sand,
And every time a locomotive goes rolling on by,
They say, "There lies a steel drivin' man,
There lies a steel drivin' man."

Sometimes slaves entertained white people with their music. Other times both races sang the same songs at the same churches. Slowly black and white music shaped each other. They started to mix together.

African music used something called call-and-response. A lead singer called out a line. Then the rest of the singers answered back. Here's an example that you may know:

Blues legend BB King sings the blues, a form of modern music that's rooted in African folk music.

THE POLKA

An example of European folk music is the polka. Polkas come from Poland and Germany. It was music meant for dancing.

Oh you can't get to Heaven
(Oh you can't get to Heaven)
On roller skates
(On roller skates)
'Cause you'll roll right past
('Cause you'll roll right past)
Those pearly gates
(Those pearly gates.)

One of the most famous types of African American music is called the blues. Blues music is very sad. It talks about sadness or loneliness. It's very simple but very powerful.

Blues music is fairly new. It became popular in the 1920s, and it is still popular today. But it has its roots in old African songs. African music also shaped other kinds of modern music, like jazz and rock and roll. America's music wouldn't be the same without Africa!

Different regions of North America use different instruments in
their folk music. Some kinds of folk music from Louisiana often

FIVE
Folk Variations

Each part of the United States has a different kind of folk music. That makes sense— people from different parts of the world ended up in each region.

Although it's all folk music, there are some differences between each one. The instruments people use are different. The sorts of words they use are different. The rhythms they use are different.

Louisiana

In the 1700s, many French people ended up in Louisiana. They mixed with Native Americans, Africans, and Hispanics in the same place. Their children were known as Cajuns.

Cajun music is **unique**. It has some influence from all the **cultures** just mentioned. Violins and accordions are important Cajun instruments. The accordion was loud enough to play music that could be hear in a crowded dance hall.

Zydeco is a popular kind of music today. It comes from Cajun, Caribbean, and blues music, all mixed together. Zydeco is faster than most Cajun music. It mostly comes out of Louisiana.

Hispanic

The Southwest of the United States has its own folk music. Some of it started out as songs cowboys sung around their campfires. Other Southwestern folk songs have Hispanic roots in Mexico.

Hispanic folk music is pretty different from other types of North American folk music. It has more in common with Native American music. Music from Spain was also an important influence.

There are different sorts of Hispanic folk music. One is the corrido. Corridos usually tell love stories. They are simple, with one singer and maybe a guitar.

Hispanic folk music uses lots of instruments. The accordion is one of the major ones. Drums, guitars, harmonicas, and violins are also used.

Folk Revival

With the invention of the radio and record players, many people started learning new music. Music was no longer something

BLUEGRASS

The term "bluegrass" music comes from the 1940s. Back then, there was a group of musicians called Bill Monroe and the Bluegrass Boys. Bill and his two brothers grew up in the Appalachian Mountains in Tennessee. They eventually moved north to Chicago and brought bluegrass music there. Bill got more and more famous. Lots of people heard them. Because of Bill Monroe and his group, bluegrass music became popular around the country.

that was only passed from person to person. Now, songs could be sold. Music became a business.

Then in the 1950s and '60s, many people wanted to listen to folk music again. People in cities and suburbs wanted to be reminded of life in the country. Folk music was simpler than the rock'n'roll and metal they could hear on the streets.

Folk music is gong to be around for a long time. When someone picks up a guitar and picks out a simple tune, lots of times he's playing a folk song. When you sing songs around a campfire, you're probably singing folk songs. When parents sing their child a lullaby, they're usually singing a folk song. Folk music will never die!

Find Out More

In Books

Feierabend, John M. *The Book of Children's Song Tales.* Chicago: Gia, 2003.

Hayden, Tim. *Children of the World: Fun Songs and Fun Facts from Many Lands.* Los Angeles: Alfred, 2009.

Rappaport, Doreen. *No More! Stories and Songs of Slave Resistance.* Somerville, Mass.: Candlewick, 2005.

————. *Nobody Gonna Turn Me 'Round: Stories and Songs of the Civil Rights Movement.* Somerville, Mass.: Candlewick, 2006.

Yarrow, Peter. *Favorite Folk Songs.* New York: Sterling, 2008.

On the Internet

American Folk songs
www.americanfolklore.net/american-folk songs.html

Folk Music of England, Scotland, Ireland, Wales and America
www.contemplator.com/folk.html

Songs from Around the World
pdmusic.org/folk.html

Index

Picture Credits

About the Author and the Consultant

Gus Snedeker is proud of his heritage as a Dutch American. He loves to study the stories and traditions of the various groups of people who helped build America. He has also written several other books in this series.

Dr. Alan Jabbour is a folklorist who served as the founding director of the American Folklife Center at the Library of Congress from 1976 to 1999. Previously, he began the grant-giving program in folk arts at the National Endowment for the Arts (1974-76). A native of Jacksonville, Florida, he was trained at the University of Miami (B.A.) and Duke University (M.A., Ph.D.). A violinist from childhood on, he documented old-time fiddling in the Upper South in the 1960s and 1970s. A specialist in instrumental folk music, he is known as a fiddler himself, an art he acquired directly from elderly fiddlers in North Carolina, Virginia, and West Virginia. He has taught folklore and folk music at UCLA and the University of Maryland and has published widely in the field.